SABOTAGE SUCCESS

Robert L. West Junior

Copyright 2017 by Robert L. West Junior.
The book author retains sole copyright
to his contributions to this book.

Published 2017.

Printed in the United States of America.

All rights reserved.

No portion of this book may be reproduced, stored in a retrieval system, or transmitted in any form or by any means – electronic, mechanical, photocopy, recording, scanning, or other – except for brief quotations in critical reviews or articles, without the prior written permission of the author.

ISBN 978-1-943650-68-2

© Can Stock Photo / kbuntu

Published by BookCrafters, Parker, CO
www.bookcrafters.net

Chapter 1

The Sabotage

Why did it happen? Why did I not see that? What in the world was I thinking? If I had known then, what I know now. Wow, what could have been! Why should other people determine if I am a success or a failure? Do these things sound familiar? Well you are not alone; this is the start of sabotaging success.

I knew I was special, but what I did not know was how special I was. I did not want to seem arrogant or braggadocios, however there had to be a better me. Therefore, the journey began. How did I find the success of my life? What is my life's work and what will that look like? All of the unanswered questions going through my mind. Therefore, one day I had the most interesting conversation with my mind, and boy did things get interesting.

All of a sudden, I found myself with a headache and did not know why. My mind told me not to worry, I would figure it out. After my mind began to solve all of my issues, the journey started. It was amazing to me how the prefect plan of life's success was so prefect in my mind. As the journey started, my mind would take these impromptu vacations. It did not take long to realize that the mind is the key to sabotage or success.

In my mind, I had based my success on what people were going to say about me. My success goals were based solely on what I wanted people to think about me. I decided that I was going to be successful because of all the naysayers who have influenced my life. This plan was right up my mind's alley. I am going to take you on a journey of sabotaging success. In my mind, this was an exciting time. I would go to bed successful, feeling good, because my mind and I had a plan. When I woke up the next morning, reality would be starring me in the face--*your plan needs action*. So I said, "If action is what I need, then action is what I am going to get."

I would start the project, and as soon as it required substance, I would try to figure out a simpler way. This was a real ingredient for sabotage. The plan and the process were good, but my mind told me it did not take all that. It was amazing how my mind would always come off vacation just before substance was needed.

This process happened over and over again. I would think, *What is wrong? Why am I not successful? I know my plan will work. I am not a bad person. I am going to try a different way.* Back to bed and my mind started telling me again how to be successful. I developed a pattern of great ideas, wonderfully planned, with no problems. Soon I discovered I was sabotaging my own success. I had to figure out why I was doing this.

I want to be successful. I want a great life. I want everybody to love me, and I have the prefect plan. I begin to quote Your gifts and make room for You. I see

I am gifted. I need room. The new plan was to make it happen in my mind, and then it would just appear. My mind told me this is a great plan. This is a plan that is fool-proof and cannot fail.

I am going to make this work and all of the naysayers are going to have to bow down to me. I'm going to get a shirt that says, "Take a look at me." I said to myself, *I am going to show everybody a picture of success.*

So every night I went to bed and my mind would be right there coaching me on my plan to be successful. My mind never would tell me about any problems that did not have a perfect outcome. I woke saying my destiny has to be successful because what other reason would You come to my mind. If I I'm not successful, it's got to be somebody else's fault. I know my plan is perfect so it has to be the naysayers, doubters, haters and satan stopping me. I could not let this happen. My mind would tell me what to do and how handle all of the negativity trying to stop me.

Chapter 2

The Plan

My plan for a successful life all started when I saw a car drive down the street. Everybody stared, and the driver just smiled. *That is going to be me one day and people are going to look at me and want to be me*, I said to myself. I would look at magazines, watch TV, have fake conversation with agents, celebrities and TV personalities. After I finished daydreaming of all the things I wanted, and what people were going to say, the plan started.

I planned my success step by step in my mind. I was going to get a great education without having to study hard. I was going to get a high paying job and be in high demand all over the over the country.

This great master plan began at the age of eleven when a young man got a taste of success. It all started on a cool fall day in the local city park where the elementary football game was taught. The eleven-year-old kid made the football team and was playing in his first game. It was an exciting time for him, He wore his uniform, with the number 40 on the front and back, and he was ready. The referees yelled with a loud voice, "Play ball."

There were people standing all around the field including the young man's parents and family members.

The parents were yelling for their children. You could smell hotdogs and hamburgers cooking in the crisp fall air. It was exciting. As the game began, the eleven-year-old boy with the number 40 on his jersey was ready to play. The coach looked around and said, "Young men, do your best, and I will be proud of you."

The game went on for three quarters and the eleven-year-old had not had a chance to play. He began to look at his parents and wonder what they were thinking. He thought, *If I don't get a chance to play, they will be so disappointed.*

As time was winding down in the game, the coach called timeout. The coach said, "We are down by five points. I believe we still have a chance, but who has not had a chance to play?"

When he said that the eleven-year-old boy raised his hand, and some of the players dropped their heads in disbelief. The coach sent in number 40, because everybody got a chance.

The boy ran onto the field excited and happy he was finally in the game. The quarterback came to the huddle, looked at him and said, "I guess you are going to run the ball." The players broke out of the huddle, and the young man looked up and saw his father smiling, clapping and pointing at him.

The quarterback said, "Hut one, hut two, hike." He pitched the ball to number 40, and he ran and ran until he made it to the end zone. Touchdown! They had won the game, and number 40 had run his first touchdown.

After the game, the young man ran to his parents so excited and ready to celebrate. For the rest of the evening he explained that he was now "the man." He said, "I bet they let me play early in the next game. The eleven-year-old young man got a taste of early success.

But, he found out that just because you do well, not everybody is happy for you.

At the next game, the first quarter came and went, and he still had not played. The second quarter, the coach looked around and said, "Where is 40?"

The young man quickly raised his hand and said, "Here I am, coach, here I am!"

Coach said, "Get in there, number 40."

The young man ran onto the field, looked at the quarterback and said, "Give me the ball, and get out the way."

The young man completed the game with five touchdowns, and a star was discovered. Now he was on his way to a successful season, as long as he did not get hurt. As the season progressed, number 40 played really well and people began to tell him to do well, do not stop, and you are special.

A week before the last game, some of the players decided to skip school to go to the store. Number 40 knew he should to go to school, but he decided to go along to get along, and he skipped school too. When they got to the store, the clerk asked them, "Shouldn't you boys be at school?"

One of the boys said, "No, we are out today."

They got some snacks and were walking down the street. The school truant officer pulled up beside them and said, "You boys are in big trouble." He put the boys in the car and took them to school where he called the boys' parents.

Number 40 sat there wondering what was going to happen. When his parents made it to the school, they were informed that 40 had been suspended from the team and could no longer play this year.

As he left with his parents, he thought, *The team cannot win without me, and they will let me play*. But that did not happen. The team won their last game, and the season was over. Forty thought, *If I had of just gone to school, I would have been on the championship team. I did it to myself.*

I was sabotaged.

Chapter 3

The Judgement

There was a young man who actually "had it all," according to what people said. He had a successful high school career participating in activities, graduating with honors, and receiving a college scholarship. After graduating from college he began his professional career as a business analyst. He was twenty-two years old. He had his own apartment, independence, excellent health, and a bright red sport car. All of his friends were jealous and envious. He had a nickname. People called him "Mr. Shine."

Well Mr. Shine would begin his day at the local coffee shop with a cappuccino. As he left the shop in his red sport car, people would look at him and smile, and that made him feel good. When Mr. Shine made it to work, he walked in his office, looked at his cherry-wood furniture and said, "I am the man."

Mr. Shine was very good at his job and made the company millions of dollars. The owner of the company recognized his talent and told his supervisor, if he kept up the good work, at the end of the year I'm going to give him a promotion. Mr. Shine's supervisor shared the good news with him.

After work Mr. Shine decided to go out and celebrate the good news he had received. He and his friends were eating and drinking, laughing and talking when one of them had a bright idea. Let's go to a club. Mr. Shine knew he did not like clubs and had not been to a club since he had left college.

His friend told him, "We won't stay long. We will just go for a couple of hours and then head home."

Mr. Shine thought, *Why not? It might be fun.*

So they went to the club and found a seat. Music was playing; people looked like they were having a good time. Time went by and they realized they had been in the club for five hours. It was four o'clock in the morning.

Mr. Shine left the club, drove out of the parking lot and was pulled over by a police car with flashing lights. The policeman asked Mr. Shine's for his driver's license, and when he reached for his wallet, he discovered it was not there. He began to explain to the officer, "I must have left it in the building."

The officer asked, "What building you are talking about?"

"The office where I work."

"Please step out of the car. Mr. Shine, have you been drinking?"

Mr. Shine said, "No sir."

The officer told Mr. Shine he smelled alcohol and asked if he would take a sobriety test. Mr. Shine refused to take the test and the police told him, "I'm going to have to take you in to the police station."

While on his way to the police station, Mr. Shine thought, *I am going to miss work, and I can't call my job and say I'm in jail.* You see, the company Mr. Shine worked for had a strict policy about integrity, after-hours activities, and criminal infractions.

Mr. Shine was finger printed and had a mug shot taken. The policeman told Mr. Shine he was being arrested for refusal to take a DUI test, driving without a license, and false pretense.

Mr. Shine asked, "Can I make a phone call?"

"You can make a phone call in an hour, when the desk sergeant gets here," the officer replied. At 10:00 a.m. Mr. Shine got his phone call, and he called the friend he went out with.

Mr. Shine's friend answered the phone and said, "Why aren't you at work? The owner of the company made a surprise visit and was asking for you. Your supervisor said you were not there and that they have not heard from you. Where are you?"

He said, "I am in jail."

"For what?"

"I got stopped by the police. I did not have my wallet, and I refused to take a sobriety test.

His friend said, "I have your wallet. I thought it was mine, but I don't know how I got it.

"Can you come and bail me out? I will pay back the money."

"Give me a couple of hours, and I will be there."

When Mr. Shine's friend arrived at the jail he said, "Man, you won't believe what happened.

Mr. Shine said, "What?"

"I got a promotion."

What a sabotage.

Chapter 4

Solution to Sabotage

We were all created to be successful. A lot of times we sabotage our own success. If we allow other people to dictate to us the flow of our life, success has a greater chance of being sabotaged. The truth of the matter is if you allow your mind to focus on action more than the purpose, you have a greater chance of sabotaging success.

This happens more than we realize. You have a successful product in yourself, which is why we must utilize it for His purpose and not just in action. People will call for actions and reactions by you; however, you must focus on the purpose. We have to make decisions based upon the purpose of the mission.

Your mission has to be grounded by your faith, and built on a foundation not made by man. If you know what you want to accomplish, ask yourself, *Will my next decision sabotage my success?*

We have to stop taking chances on our success and stay focused on the mission. You have to know what you want to accomplish and not let temporary pleasures, rash decisions, and outside influences, make you lose focus. One thing these people had in common was, they had a choice to make a better decision.

If you know that you are a good product, then why let a naysayer, non-encourager, negative influence, or just someone who doesn't want to see you succeed, have a say? You must realize that you will not sabotage your success for a snack at a store, a night out on the town, or your own personal ego. The purpose is too important to sabotage success. You must continue to make good decisions, wise choices that benefit the purpose.

Sometimes we lose focus on what was really important. Life is not always about what people think of you, but it is about what you want GOD to think of you. Of course, God loves us and that is why He created us to succeed. Furthermore, He continues to give us the chance not to sabotage our success. Do not sabotage your success. Please!

About the Author

Robert West Jr. was born to Dr. Robert West Sr. and Dr. Linda Jones-West in a small Mississippi town. From the beginning of his life, he knew he was destined to serve people. As he participated in different activities, organizations, church functions, and community service projects, his service resume began. His inspiration for writing this book or was to help people realize what took him several years to accept: he was created to serve. His wife, Pia Green-West, and daughter, Linbethany West, drive the service journey.

I believe I am a common person with a divine purpose to serve others and help people understand how to not sabotage success in life. What I have learned after losing 206 pounds, and still counting, you really do not have to sabotage success.

www.ingramcontent.com/pod-product-compliance
Lightning Source LLC
Chambersburg PA
CBHW020034120526
44588CB00030B/440